CW00393721

If you grow any vegetables in your garden then runner beans are likely to be among them. We all love the arrival of the crisp tender pods in mid-summer, but soon the ubiquitous phrase "Please no more…." rings out across the country. I present here sixty recipes to help you enjoy Britain's favourite vegetable. With increasing concerns about sustainability, global warming, and more immediately, the credit crunch there has never been a time better to start to use this prolific garden vegetable in more imaginative ways.

The Runner Bean Cook Book

Simon Taylor

S J Taylor

SJT

The Runner Bean Cook Book
Copyright © 2009 Simon Taylor

First published in Sheffield, Great Britain

S J Taylor
http://myweb.tiscali.co.uk/herbandsexdiet

All rights reserved. No part of this publication may be reproduced, stored in a retrieval system, or transmitted in any form or by any means, electronic, mechanical, photocopying, recording or otherwise, without the prior permission of the author or the publisher.

ISBN 978-0-9553954-1-3

Illustrations: Simon Taylor,
Designer: Simon Taylor

Printed by Lightning Source UK Ltd

To Alison, John
and Eleanor

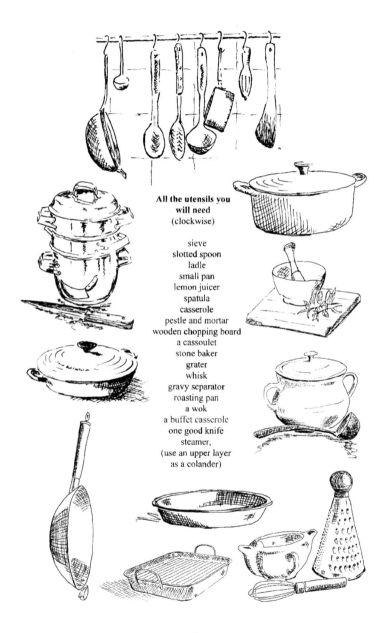

**All the utensils you
will need**
(clockwise)

sieve
slotted spoon
ladle
small pan
lemon juicer
spatula
casserole
pestle and mortar
wooden chopping board
a cassoulet
stone baker
grater
whisk
gravy separator
roasting pan
a wok
a buffet casserole
one good knife
steamer,
(use an upper layer
as a colander)

6

Contents

Introduction

Phaseolus coccineus

We all welcome runner beans, as the salad leaves in the garden start take a turn for the worse. Served with sage butter, freshly ground black pepper, warm home baked bread and a glass of crisp grassy white wine, they make a perfect starter. Eaten at the close of a hot summer day, there could be few sensations that could be so quintessentially English. Unfortunately the magic soon fades. This is not surprising as runner beans are easy to grow, however cack-handed you are in the garden, and there are enough seeds in the average packet to produce a crop of 25 to 30kg! They are brilliant with the Sunday roast but if you pick them only once a week they will disappoint, as more full grown and tougher beans will develop. These are not only less palatable but will turn off the flower producing mechanism of the plant so that three Sundays after your first meal the supply of firm young tender beans will be over. One solution that some books suggest is continuing to pick in the week and throw these unused ones away. What a waste; runner beans are a rich source of vitamin C, folic acid and fibre and at less than twenty calories per hundred grams there is much more that we can do with them.

Chelsea Physic Garden

Runner beans are perennial plants in their native cool high-altitude regions of central and northern South America. Wild small podded plants still grow in cool partially shaded valleys of mixed pine and oak in Guatemala and Mexico. Evidence from Mexican caves suggests their use as a food stuff 6000 years ago with domestication and cultivation for the last 2000 years. Not only are the pods eaten but also the roots. I would not recommend the latter either boiled or roasted as they taste a bit like a bland starchy parsnip.

Runner beans were introduced to Europe following the return of Columbus after his second voyage to the New World and spread from Spain into the eastern Mediterranean. They are first listed in England by John Tradescant, gardener to Charles I, in 1634 but were initially only grown as a decorative plant. It was a century later when Philip Miller, keeper of Chelsea Physic Garden, became the first to cook and eat them here.

Autumn frosts in the UK have their annual cull, but fortunately runner beans are among the easiest vegetables to grow. Most seeds will germinate, but spring frosts remain a danger. One unhelpful suggestion is to plant the seeds one week before the last frost, whenever that would be! Another is that planting the seeds on the night of Good Friday brings good luck, but if there is a frost three weeks later, your seedlings will be dead and you will have to start again. I prefer to sow in 7.5cm pots in April which also protects the tender plants from slugs.

Plant out in a sunny spot when you know the frosts have passed, about 30cm between plants. All but dwarf plants will need support. There are the traditional wigwams or paired rows of canes triangulated at the top. Some people use an existing fence or arch, taking advantage of their decorative nature. Generally the plants will be free of diseases although planting Marigolds nearby apparently attracts insects which will harvest any black fly that may dare to even contemplate your beans. The idea of companion planting is not new and back in their native South America beans are planted with maize and squashes. The maize provides support for the beans and the ground hugging squash provide a living mulch which retains moisture and suppresses weeds. The beans, being part of the *legume* family of vegetables, have bacteria in their roots which fixes nitrogen from the air, so providing a natural nitrogen fertilizer for all the plants. The care of your beans at home is not difficult. Pinch out the growing point when it has reached the top of the poles, and keep the soil weed free and moist. It is during a dry patch, when I am hiking yet another watering can over to my beans, that I think that next year the effort would be better spent preparing the soil properly and digging in lots of moisture retaining organic material.

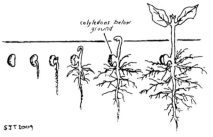

cotyledons below ground

SJT 2009

Your toils will soon be rewarded and you will have a crop. The beans are at their best when fresh, young, tender, snap easily and not full length. Cropping every few days encourages new flowers and a continued supply. So which of the many varieties should you grow? Although the Royal Horticultural Society have recently extensively tested forty eight, I have restricted myself to those varieties easily available on the high street or average garden centre and concentrated on texture and flavour only.

Variety	Flower colour	Texture	Taste
Scarlet Emperor	Red	Softens up quickly	Nice home-grown and earthy flavour
Streamline	Red	Squeaky	A little bitter
Polestar	Red	Good	Bland
Prizewinner Stringless	Red	Chewy	Dry and bitter
Enorma	White	Good	A bit flat
Painted Lady	White faced flowers with red painted lips	Juicy but slightly squeaky	Fruity, nice but beaten by Lady Di
Lady Di, Stringless	Red		Archetypal, as you remember the first pick of the crop
Czar	White	Soft	Little flavour

13

In the tradition of blind tastings the list is not extensive and subjective although my favourite, Lady Di, achieved an Award of Garden Merit from the RHS.

In the kitchen I do not follow the advice that you should remove the stringy bits down each side of the bean even on the non stringless varieties. This is too much effort. If your beans are young and fresh enough, all you need to do is top and tail and slice the beans up at an acute diagonal angle. If you want to remove the stringy bits then use a vegetable peeler. I would not store the beans, even in the vegetable compartment of the fridge, as their sweetness is lost within days as the natural sugars are converted to starch. You can freeze the prepared beans but my advice here is put them in food containers. The acute angle of the frozen bean is quite sharp enough to lacerate the average freezer bag with the inevitable consequence that you will soon have free-range beans everywhere in your freezer.

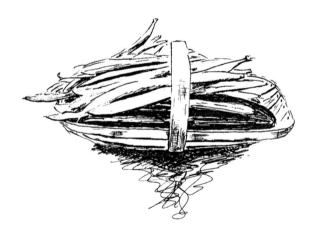

The recipes in this book are all relatively simple, in fact some involve little more than combining the ingredients in a dish and baking them. I think this is important. Good food can be easy to prepare and enjoyed by everyone with very little more thought, effort or skill than preparing packaged, so called instant food. Even if you have only ever done toast before, have a go. We all make mistakes and things go wrong, but with the use of tasty fresh ingredients this is seldom a complete disaster. Be organised in the kitchen; get out what you need and think through what you are going to do before you start. I also think you really need to be in the mood to cook so that you can do it with love and passion. And don't be afraid to experiment.

Happy
Cooking

Recipes

Steaming and blanching

I blanch my beans for about one to two minutes in boiling water and strain. I steam my beans for as little as five minutes and certainly no more than ten, really depending on how young and tender they are. You can judge for yourself when you feel the texture is right.

The general recommendation is that beans should be cooked. This is because of a natural chemical called phytohaemagglutinin which is what makes uncooked red kidney beans poisonous. Most of it is destroyed by cooking. Runner beans do have this, but in a fraction of the amount, and it is only in the beans as opposed to the pods. In addition the plants do not start producing it until at least two and a half weeks after the flowers are fertilized. Eating the youngest, most tender pods uncooked should therefore cause no problems. I like to pick a pod as I pass and munch it walking down the garden, like an apple. I have occasionally used uncooked beans in some of the recipes below.

Starters

Crostini

There are five combinations here. Finely chop the ingredients and mix with the oil and finely grated cheese and leave at room temperature for at least half an hour. Cut French bread into one centimetre thick slices and toast. If you use a toaster, stand them up on the crust while you toast the next lot so the toast does not go soft. Then pile with the topping. A perfect lunch, either with really cold European lager or dry white or rose wine. The variable that is difficult to predict, but still important, is the sun. Despite the garlic and the Parmesan, there are delicate flavours here and their consumption in the open summer air is as an important ingredient as any.

one

Sorrel leaves
Uncooked young beans
Sage leaves
Parmesan, grated
Small onion
Salt and pepper
Olive oil

two

Blanched beans
Crushed garlic
Mint leaves
Salt and pepper
Parmesan, grated
Olive oil

three

Uncooked young beans
Small tomato
A small fraction of a red onion
Coriander leaves
Lemon juice
Olive oil

four

Blanched beans
Half a roasted red pepper
Basil leaves

Half a dozen black olives
Salt and pepper
Olive oil

five

Black olives
Parsley
Half a clove of garlic, crushed
Teaspoon of capers
Blanched beans
Salt and pepper
Olive oil

Fresh bean soup

Ingredients (for 4)

240g runner beans, sliced
1l chicken stock, p 80.
1 bunch of mint
1 bunch of parsley
1 teaspoon tarragon, chopped
Salt and freshly ground black pepper
60g angel hair spaghetti, broken into 3cm lengths
Basil leaves, olive oil and Parmesan shavings to serve

Make a bouquet with the mint and parsley. Bring the stock to the boil with the bouquet and when boiling throw in the beans and tarragon. Season to taste. Put in the pasta to cook for the appropriate amount of time and remove the bouquet to serve. Serve with basil leaves, parmesan and a drizzle with olive oil.

Oriental runner bean soup

Ingredients (for 4)

240g runner beans, sliced
60g long grain rice
1l chicken stock, p 80.
1 onion, finely chopped
2cm cube ginger, cut into fine strips
3 tablespoons (45ml) juice of 2 lemons
1 pot of coriander, chopped
Salt and pepper to taste

Bring the stock to the boil with the onion and rice and cook until the rice is almost cooked, about 10 minutes. Throw in the beans and continue for three to four minutes until the beans are just tender and throw in the ginger and the lemon juice. Season. Serve with coriander.

Do not be tempted to do any soup that involves food processing the beans. This produces a metallic back taste to the soup.

Cold meat and beans with tapenade

Ingredients (for 4)

40 - 50 black olives
3 - 4 anchovy fillets
1 garlic clove
Freshly ground black pepper
1 small handful of basil leaves
2 - 3 dessertspoons (20ml - 30ml) olive oil

Crush everything in a pestle, mix in the oil and leave in the fridge overnight. Tear up pieces of cold meat, left over from the Sunday roast, and toss with lightly steamed beans and as much of the tapenade as you like. Serve with fresh crusty bread.

Crunchy bean and chicken salad

Ingredients (for 4)

2 slices of sliced white bread, toasted, and cut into soldiers
Zest of one orange
An anchovy fillet for each soldier
Parmesan cheese
Olive oil
1 roast chicken breast, shredded
300g - 400g runner beans, sliced
1 - 2 dessertspoons (10ml - 20ml) juice of one lemon

Not too precise on the quantities here. Put the soldiers on a small baking tray. Divide the orange zest between the soldiers, place an anchovy fillet on each, grate a little parmesan and drizzle with olive oil. Bake until crispy, a bit like fried bread. When cool enough break into large crumbs. Mix the shredded cooked chicken breast with lightly steamed beans and serve by sprinkling with these crumbs, black pepper and the lemon juice.

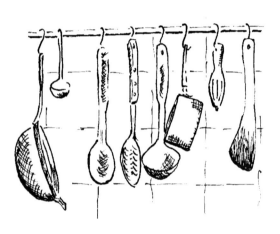

Fish

Baked cod with runner beans and pancetta

Ingredients (for 4)

600g - 800g runner beans, sliced
1 garlic clove, very finely sliced or crushed
Salt and pepper
1 tablespoon (15ml) olive oil
Four 225g cod steaks (or 600g cod loin if, like my children, you don't like bones)
12 slices of pancetta or equivalent dry smoked ham
One handful of pine nuts
Two lemons, quartered

Basically mix all the beans, salt and pepper and oil in a baking tray and put on top of this the fish wrapped in the ham. Put in the lemons. Throw in the pine nuts and place in a preheated oven at 220°C for 15 minutes. The fish is cooked when it comes off the bone easily. Pour the juices from the pan over the beans and fish when you serve. Devour with loads of crusty bread washed down with icy Sauvignon Blanc.

Baked salmon with runner beans

This is another family favourite and it gets my children to eat green things!

Ingredients (for 4)

600g - 800g runner beans, sliced
20 cherry tomatoes
Salt and pepper
1 tablespoon (15ml) olive oil
1 handful of black olives
Four 225g salmon steaks
1 tin of anchovy fillets
1 handful of basil leaves
2 lemons

Basically as above (*Baked cod with runner beans and pancetta*) but lay the anchovies over the beans and tomatoes. Season the salmon skin so it can crisp. Squeeze the juice of one of the lemons over before cooking and serve with the other lemon just quartered.

Trout with black pudding

1 trout per person, gutted
And per fish
150g - 200g runner beans, sliced
100g black pudding, 1cm thick slices
1 apple, 1cm slices
3 sprigs of sage, finely chop the leaves of one of these sprigs
1 dessertspoon (10ml) juice of half a lemon
Salt and pepper
Icing sugar

Blanch the beans. Lightly sauté the black pudding. Mix the beans, black pudding, the chopped sage leaves and lemon juice in an oven proof dish. Place the other two sprigs of sage in the seasoned cavity of the trout and place it on the beans. Place the apple round the fish to fill the gaps. Season the trout skins with salt and pepper so they go crispy and lightly sprinkle the sugar on the apples so they caramelise. Bake at 180°C for about 20 - 25 minutes or until the fish easily comes off the bone.

Sweet and sour mackerel with beans

1 mackerel per person, filleted
and per mackerel
3 pickled chillies, p 76.
3 small pieces of preserved lemon, p 75.
1 - 2 teaspoons (5ml - 10ml) Soya sauce
1 sweet potato, peeled, 2cm slices
150g - 200g runner beans, sliced

Roughly chop the chillies and lemon, sprinkle with half the Soya sauce and stuff the mackerel with this mixture, tying each fillet up with three to five loops of string and leave for about an hour. Par boil the potato and blanch the beans. Drain the beans and put in an oven proof dish with the mackerel on top and sprinkle with the rest of the Soya sauce. Fill the gaps around and between the fish with the potato pieces, brush with oil and lightly dust the lot with salt and pepper. Bake at 180°C for 20 minutes.

Mackerel with root vegetables and runner beans

Ingredients (for 4)

4 mackerel, gutted
1 onion, finely chopped
2 carrots, cut into julienne strips
2 parsnips, cut into julienne strips
400g - 500g runner beans, sliced
1 small knob of butter (15g)
Small bunch of parsley, chopped

1 thyme sprig, leaves removed and chopped
Freshly ground black pepper and salt
2 dessertspoons of capers, rinsed
1 tomato, peeled and chopped
100ml white wine

Sauté the carrots and onions in the butter until just starting to go soft and then add the beans for a couple of minutes. Mix in the herbs, tomato, black pepper, capers and white wine and pour the lot into an oven proof dish. Put the fish on top. Liberally sprinkle the skin of the fish with salt so it goes crisp. Bake at 180°C for 20 to 30 minutes until the fish easily comes away from the bone.

A variant of fish cassoulet

Ingredients (for 4)

150g white fish, 2cm cube
150g salmon, 2cm cube
1 can haricot beans/butter beans, drained
300g runner beans, sliced
2 tomatoes, chopped
1 leek, finely sliced
1 head of garlic, separated and skinned
1 tablespoon (15ml) olive oil
Salt and pepper
1 chilli, finely chopped
2 dessertspoons (20ml) juice of one lemon
1 cup of breadcrumbs
25g grated cheese
Boiling water

Put all the ingredients into a cassoulet or high sided casserole except the breadcrumbs and cheese. Add boiling water to almost cover the surface. Bake covered for 10 minutes at 180°C. Uncover and sprinkle on breadcrumbs and cheese and continue to bake for twenty minutes or until the breadcrumbs are golden.

Meat

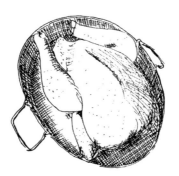

Breakfast beans

Not really a light breakfast but if you are walking all day it makes a great start. You will need a small frying pan (about ten inches diameter). You cook one portion at a time and the quantities are per head.

About 50g of each:
      Chorizo, cut into lardons
      Smoked bacon lardons
      Black pudding, ½cm slices
100g runner beans, sliced
½ red pepper, cut into 2cm squares

1 egg
1 pinch of paprika
1 pinch black pepper
1 teaspoon cumin seeds, dry roasted in the pan before you start on the rest
1 teaspoon (5ml) olive oil

Sauté the meats in the oil for about one minute and throw in the beans and red pepper. Cook slowly for about 10 minutes before adding spices and toss the contents over for about a minute before breaking the egg on top. Cook the egg to the consistency you like and serve with crusty bread and a cold beer.

Lamb stew with runner beans

Ingredients (for 2)

200g lamb, fat trimmed off, 2cm cube
1 onion, sliced
200g potatoes, 1cm slice
200g - 300g runner beans, sliced
300g tomatoes, diced
1 handful of basil leaves, roughly torn
1 handful of coriander, roughly chopped
½ - 1 teaspoon black pepper coarsely crushed
½ - 1 teaspoon paprika
Salt

This is low effort. Put everything except the beans in a casserole and just cover with water. Cover and place in an oven at 180°C for 40 minutes. Now check the liquid level, add the beans and return to the oven for another 40 minutes.

Polish beans

Ingredients (for 4)

400g - 500g runner beans, sliced
1 can of cannellini beans, drained and rinsed
1 spring onion, finely chopped
½ tin of anchovy fillets, drained and chopped
1 can of frankfurters, heated through
2 eggs, hard boiled
Pinch of paprika
1 tablespoon (15ml) white wine vinegar
1 tablespoon (15ml) olive oil
Salt and pepper

Steam the beans and put into a warmed salad bowl. Add cannellini beans, spring onions and anchovies. Season with salt and pepper, mix and place the warmed frankfurters on top. Chop eggs, mix with paprika and season with salt and pepper. Add the vinegar and olive oil. Dress the beans and sausage with this sauce.

Tagine aux haricot coccineus

A good thing to do as the bean season comes to an end and the beans are losing flavour and tenderness.

Ingredients (for 4)

500g stewing beef, 2 - 3cm cube
1 onion, chopped
1 tablespoon (15ml) olive oil
1 tomato, skinned and diced
4 cloves garlic, crushed
Salt
¼ teaspoon freshly ground black pepper
½ teaspoon ground ginger
A pinch of saffron
A little water
500g runner beans, sliced
2 courgettes, cut into sticks the same size as the beans
A handful each of parsley and coriander, chopped
2 dessertspoons (20ml - 25ml) juice of one lemon

Sauté onions in the olive oil until translucent and seal the beef. Add tomato, garlic, salt, pepper, ginger, saffron and a little water to just cover. Cover the casserole and bake at 150°C for 45 minutes before adding the beans and courgettes. Cook for a further twenty minutes before adding the lemon juice and three quarters of the parsley and coriander, reserving the remainder to serve. Cook for another ten minutes. Serve with couscous.

North African minced beef with runner beans

Ingredients (for 4)

400g minced beef
400g runner beans, sliced
1 onion, chopped
1 teaspoon nutmeg
1 teaspoon cinnamon
1 teaspoon black pepper
1 teaspoon salt
25g raisons
25g currants
50g dried apricots, chopped
1 handful of parsley, chopped

Mix the mince with the spices, salt and pepper. In a heavy based pan with a lid sauté the onion until it starts to become translucent. Throw in the mince and stir fairly vigorously so that the mince does not clump and each bit starts to brown without it sticking to its neighbour. Now throw in the dried fruit, beans and parsley, mix and cover. Simmer, covered, for about fifteen minutes to allow the spices to infuse. Serve with pittas, yoghurt and chilli flakes or sauce.

Stir fried chicken with peanut sauce

Ingredients (for 4)

200g chicken breast, thinly sliced
150g runner beans, sliced
150g carrots, cut into julienne strips
30g kale, stems removed and cut into strips
and for the marinade
2 cloves garlic, crushed
1 red chilli, finely chopped
2cm cube of fresh ginger, finely chopped
½ teaspoon ground coriander
½ teaspoon black pepper
2 dessertspoon (20 - 25ml) juice of one lemon
1 tablespoon (15ml) Soya sauce
and to serve
1 tablespoon sesame seeds dry roasted in a frying pan
and for the peanut sauce
4 tablespoons of peanut butter
1 dessertspoon (10ml) Soya sauce
1 dessertspoon (10ml) runny honey
4 tablespoons (60ml) water

Marinate the chicken while you prepare the vegetables
and make the peanut sauce. In a small pan gently warm
the ingredients for the peanut sauce. It will look a mess
as you start but as you blend it becomes a smooth sauce.
Turn off the heat well before allowing it to bubble. Heat
a little oil in a wok and seal the chicken. Add the beans
and carrot and cook until al denté. Now add the kale and
marinade and continue to cook on a lower heat for three

to four minutes. Serve with noodles, sprinkled with the sesame seeds and the peanut sauce on the side.

Brittany chicken

This is a derivative of a Brittany dish. This is a good evening meal as the bean season comes to an end and they start to get a bit tougher. Serve with roast potatoes.

Ingredients (for 4)

1 small chicken, jointed, p38, keep the carcass for stock
75g smoked bacon, diced
12 small onions or shallots
1 carrot, sliced
400g runner beans, sliced
200ml white wine
2 lettuces, like little gem, quartered
1 teaspoon of chopped thyme leaves
1 teaspoon of chopped winter savory leaves or twice as much tarragon
1 bay leaf
Salt and pepper

Ideally use a buffet casserole (a shallow enamelled cast iron casserole) for this. Season the chicken and seal it in the oil. Remove the chicken from the pan and throw in the onions, carrot and bacon. When the onion starts to look a little translucent, return the chicken to the pan along with the beans, herbs, lettuce, wine and salt and pepper. Cover and place in an oven at 170°C for 45 - 50 minutes.

To joint a bird; locate the breast bone and cut away the breast meat on one side working towards the wing joint. When you reach this, cut through it. Cut this piece in two so you have a breast and a wing. Locate, using your fingers, the joint where the leg joins the body and pull it away from the body so you can see the joint and then cut through it. Cut the leg in two at the knee joint. Do the same on the other side and you have eight joints and a carcass. Freeze the carcass to make stock, p80.

Tray baked belly pork and runner beans

This is a meal in one dish for four.

500g belly pork as lean as you can get
500g runner beans, sliced
300g potatoes, par boiled and sliced
2 lemons, zest and juice of one and the other cut it into 2mm - 3mm slices
1 tomato, chopped
1 small onion, finely chopped
1 handful of sage, most finely chopped
¼ teaspoon black pepper
Maldon salt
10g - 15g butter

Lightly grease a small baking dish which will just fit the pork and throw in a few sage leaves. Score the skin of the pork, spread half the butter on it and rub in salt. Add 150ml water and carefully cover the dish with foil ensuring that it does not touch the skin but makes a good seal to keep the steam in as it cooks. Cook at 150°C for two and a half hours. Layer potatoes in another lightly greased baking dish. Mix all the other ingredients except the lemon slices and put on top of the potatoes. Remove pork and place on top of the beans with small knob of extra butter and a twist more salt to the skin. Separate the fluids in the first dish to remove fat and add this stock with a couple of tablespoons of water and cover the remaining exposed beans with the lemon slices. Bake at 200°C for three quarters of an hour.

Boiled ham with vegetables

This is derived from a French recipe but France is too warm to grow runners. There is an amalgamation of richness and the slower you cook the ham the better. This is a cheap meal as you will have enough to feed six and have about a litre of ham stock for soup as well! It is so warming when there is a chilled winter wind howling outside, so it is a good use of some of your frozen beans. Serve it up in large bowls with a glass of ale or Beaujolais in front of a log fire.

Ingredients (for 6)

3 large onions or 5 small, chopped
2 - 3 leeks, sliced

2 ham hocks, about 1kg each
½ - 1 cabbage, cut into sixths or eighths
4 carrots, 2cm lengths
1 - 2 parsnips, 2cm lengths
300g - 400g potatoes, 2cm cubes
100g - 200g peas
200g runner beans, sliced
200g haricot beans, soaked overnight
3 - 4 cloves
3 - 4 cloves garlic, finely sliced
1 bay leaf
1 handful of winter savory (optional)
1 dessertspoon of lovage seeds (optional)
½ teaspoon nutmeg
1 teaspoon black pepper corns, freshly crushed
½ a French loaf, (you can use yesterday's stale one), 2cm slices
Coarse French wholegrain mustard
1 tablespoon (15ml) grape seed oil, or other cooking oil

You will need a large cast iron casserole for this one. Fry the onions slowly until they are caramelised and oak brown. Add the leeks for a couple of minutes and then the ham. Cover with boiling water (this will be about two litres), cover and put in an oven at 130°C for three to four hours. Check the fluid level a couple of times during this time and top up if necessary. Remove from the oven while you vigorously boil the haricot beans for ten minutes in unsalted water and drain. At this point carefully ladle off about half (about 1 litre) of the stock letting the surface fat come over the lip of the ladle as you remove it. (The fat will float so you can remove it with the excess stock.) Add the drained haricot beans along with the cabbage, carrots, parsnip, garlic, cloves, herbs, nutmeg and pepper and replace in the oven, with the lid back on, for about three quarters of an hour. Now add the potatoes, peas and runner beans. You may need to push them down into the liquid so they are covered or add a little of the reserved stock and then return to the oven for half an hour. Slice the bread and spread each slice with a little mustard. Remove the casserole from the oven and put on a low hob while the oven temperature reaches 180°C. Arrange the bread on top, mustard side down, drizzle with a little olive oil and replace the lid until the oven is hot enough and finally bake with the lid off for five to ten minutes until the bread becomes a crispy topping. Although this sounds long winded, there is nothing else you need to do and there is plenty of time between stages to do other things while you house fills with mouth watering aromas.

This really is comfort food!

Lamb with real mint sauce

The first of a series of roasts. Lightly steamed beans complements all these, but the succulence of the sweet roast spring lamb set off by the piquancy of fresh mint sauce is probably the best. Into a roasting pan, put a sliced onion and a carrot and 250ml of water. Rub the skin of the lamb joint deeply with salt so it crisps off. Place in a preheated oven at 180°C. You can work out the time needed by allowing twenty minutes plus twenty per pound (in general I can't get rule of thumb to work with metric measures). Keep the liquid in the bottom of the pan topped up as this will be used to make the gravy. Allow fifteen minutes to let the meat relax before carving so transfer the meat onto a heated plate and cover with foil for fifteen minutes to complete your preparations, including the gravy.

Gravy

To make the gravy you will need a gravy separator. This allows you the separate the fat from all the glorious juices that have come out of the joint. In a small pan heat a dessert spoon of corn flour or plain flour in a teaspoon of butter to make a paste. Add the separated pan juices, mixing all the time so as to avoid lumps and leave to simmer and thicken while you do something else.

And mint sauce does not come in a jar from the supermarket, p 79.

Roast chicken

Roast chicken is a favourite but all too often stuffed with some re-hydrated gloop, the packet for which probably has as much flavour as its contents. This stuffed chicken however is cracking.

200g breadcrumbs
3 shallots, finely chopped
Large bunches each of parsley, dill and mint, chopped
1 small knob of butter or olive oil
Grated rind of one lemon
1 dessertspoon (10ml) fragrant Greek honey
10 black olives, chopped
Salt and black pepper

and a small to medium chicken

Sweat down shallots in the butter or oil and mix with the other ingredients. Stuff the chicken and weigh it. Prepare the roasting pan as for the lamb. Roast at 180°C for twenty minutes plus twenty minutes per pound (total weight including stuffing). You can check if it is done by inserting a skewer between the leg and the breast. If the juice runs clear then it is cooked. Remove to a hot plate to relax and continue as above to make gravy etc.

Beef with Yorkshire puddings

I prefer my beef still pink in the middle. Prepare the roasting pan as for the lamb. Place in a preheated oven at 200°C for half an hour and turn it down to 170°C. The total time will work out at twenty minutes per pound. Keep the liquid in the bottom of the pan topped up and this will make the best gravy using the same method as for the lamb but adding a drop of red wine or port makes it even richer.

For the Yorkshire puddings, ingredients (for 4)

125g plain flour
2 eggs
300ml milk
A pinch of salt
1 tablespoon (15ml) oil

Sift the flour into a mixing bowl with the salt, make a well in the middle and break in the eggs. Add half the milk and gradually work it in with a wooden spoon until it is smooth. Then beat in the rest of the milk until the surface of the mixture is covered with bubbles. I use a stone baker in which you can use a minimum of oil. Alternatively use a baking tin roughly 18cm square. Heat it with the oil in an oven at 220°C. Pour in the batter and bake for about 40 minutes.

Pork with apple sauce

Much the same as above but it is important to ensure that the meat is cooked through. Deeply score the skin and rub with melted butter and Maldon salt. Put in a preheated oven at 200°C and then turn it down after twenty minutes to 180°C. You can work out the time needed by allowing twenty minutes plus twenty minutes per pound. Once you have removed the meat to relax remove the crackling, which can still be a bit limp at this point, before covering the meat with foil. Return the crackling to the oven, just pop on top of the potatoes, to crisp off. The apple sauce is simple, p 79.

Roast potatoes (traditional)

Ingredients (for 4)

You need fluffy potatoes such as Désirée, Maris Piper or King Edward for this. These potatoes come with a health warning for two reasons. Firstly they are cooked in animal fat which makes them really crispy and secondly they are so scrumptious it is difficult to stop eating them.

You will need 750g of potatoes. Peel and cut into five to six centimetre chunks. Par boil in water with a teaspoon of salt. In the mean time heat two tablespoons of goose or duck fat or failing that lard in a baking tray. When the potatoes just start to break up at the corners, drain and add to the hot fat, turning them over to coat them. Roast at 220°C for 40 minute, turning a couple more times in the meantime to keep them basted.

yum yum !

Roast potatoes with rosemary and garlic (low fat)

Ingredients (for 4)

The rosemary and garlic are great together and the crispness of the potatoes and rosemary leaves contrasts well with the soft garlic.

600g potatoes, cut into 1 - 2cm cubes, or chips 0.5 - 1cm sections
8 - 12 cloves garlic, leave the skins on
Salt and black pepper
1 large handful rosemary, some chopped finely but leave the majority of the leaves whole
Olive oil

Mix together all the ingredients and add just enough oil to lightly coat the contents of the bowl. Spread out in one layer on the bottom of a stone or terracotta baker and cook for half an hour to 40 minutes at 180°C.

Lastly, this is such an English dish, so brilliant with runner beans and so often ignored, that I just have to include it.

Stuffed marrow

Ingredients (for 4)

This is a great meal. Don't bother though unless you have seen the marrow growing and you can testify to its freshness. Serve this with steamed runner beans and baked tomatoes and it usurps cucumber sandwiches as the quintessential taste of the English summer.

1 marrow, peeled, split lengthways and seeds scooped out.
250g minced pork
150g chorizo, finely chopped if you don't have a mincer

1 slice of white bread, crumbed (it is easier to do this if you keep frozen sliced bread and crumb it while frozen on a grater)
1 tablespoon black olives, sliced
1 dessertspoon sun dried tomato paste
1 teaspoon finely grated orange peel
1 small onion, finely chopped
1 small bunch of mint, finely chopped
1 small bunch of parsley, finely chopped
1 small egg, beaten
Salt and black pepper
½ teaspoon paprika
A pinch of cayenne pepper

Combine the ingredients in a bowl and bind them together with an egg. Place the mixture in the cavity of the marrow, making a sausage onto which the other half of the marrow is placed. Wrap tightly in buttered foil. Place on a baking tray in a preheated oven at 180°C for about an hour. The marrow should be soft when the foil is prodded.

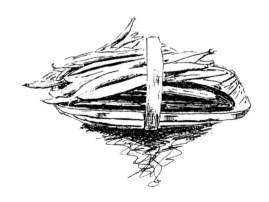

Rice and Wheat

Runner bean pizza

Ingredients (for 2)

For the base
300g strong bread flour
½ sachet of bread yeast
1 teaspoon sugar
1 pinch of salt
200ml tepid (30 - 40°C) water

and the topping
10 runner beans, sliced
½ tin anchovies
1 tablespoon tomato paste to spread on pizza base
6 black olives, pitted and halved
3 - 4 mint leaves
3 - 4 sage leaves
40g cheese, a proportion blue, grated

Work together the base ingredients with your fingers and once it becomes a dough, knead it for ten to fifteen minutes. Leave it in a warm place to rise for half an hour, covering the bowl. If you use cling film, lightly oil it since this dough is tenaciously sticky. In reality, I don't like to make unnecessary effort and use a bread machine to make my dough. The quantities above will make two bases. Turn out onto a floured work surface (I find a mixture of plain and polenta flour is best) and divide the dough in two. Roll each one out to about one centimetre thick. Place on a baking stone or tray. You can freeze the second base for another day. Italian pizzas are not piled high with topping so the quantities are ample. Whack into an oven at 190°C for fifteen minutes.

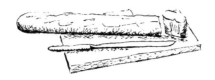

Walnut, bean and blue cheese pasta

A classic combination of walnuts and blue cheese. Serve with a peppery salad of rocket or watercress.

Ingredients (for 4)

200g - 250g of a pasta of your choice that takes about 10 minutes to cook
200g - 250g runner beans, sliced
2 handfuls of walnuts, dry roast in a frying pan until they just start to change to a golden brown
1 garlic clove, crushed
100g of a blue cheese such as stilton, crumbled
Black pepper
1 handful of parsley, chopped, divide the stalks from the leaves
50ml single cream
1 dessertspoon (10ml) of oil such as grape seed

Cook the pasta with the beans in lightly salted water. Meanwhile sauté the garlic and parsley stalks. Add the black pepper and then two tablespoons (30ml) of the cooking liquid from the pasta and mix round with a spatula to make an emulsion. Add the drained pasta and beans along with the cheese and nuts. Mix round maintaining a low heat and cover for two minutes. Mix in the cream and serve.

Carbonara

This is beautifully rich without the need to use cream as many carbonara recipes suggest.

Ingredients (for 4)

1 packet (about 225g) of smoked streaky bacon, cut into 3cm lengths
2 eggs
50g Parmesan, finely grated
Freshly ground black pepper
300g spaghetti
200g runner beans, sliced
4 cloves garlic, finely sliced
2 dessertspoons (20ml) olive oil

You do need to think about the timing for this one so that the bacon and spaghetti are ready at the same time. Start frying the bacon in the olive oil and put on the spaghetti and the beans in salted water. Warm a large mixing bowl with boiling water. As the bacon starts to crisp throw in the garlic and black pepper. Dry the bowl. Lightly beat the two eggs in the bowl with the cheese. Add the drained spaghetti and beans to the bowl and immediately mix round. (you don't want scrambled egg stuck at the bottom). Now empty all the contents of the frying pan into the bowl and stir round again. Serve immediately into warm pasta bowls with a peppery salad, crusty bread and lashings of cheap red table wine.

Risotto with beans, courgettes and parsnip

Parsnips in risotto are so creamy and rich. You may prefer this as a starter for four rather than a main course for two. This is an unconventional but low effort method of making risotto.

80g of risotto rice
1 medium parsnip, cut into julienne strips
100g runner beans, sliced
1 small courgette, cut into julienne strips
½ leek, sliced
10g of butter
25g of Parmesan cheese, grated
Freshly ground black pepper
350ml chicken stock, p80, hot
Lemon wedges to serve

You will need a pan with a lid that can go in the oven like a buffet casserole. Sauté the leek in the butter until it starts to colour. Now add the rice and mix around so that each grain has some butter coating and then add the stock. Stir round once, put on the lid and put in an oven at 150°C for twenty minutes. Now add the vegetables and cheese and a little more fluid if it looks at all dry. Stir. Replace the lid and put back in the oven for a further fifteen minutes. Serve with lemon wedges.

Paella

Ingredients (for 4)

1 leek or an onion finely chopped
1 red pepper, cut into 2cm squares
4 cloves garlic, thinly sliced
250g chicken breast, cubed
200g long grain rice
500ml chicken stock, p80, hot
200g runner beans, sliced
200g mixed seafood, prawns, mussels, squid etc
Pinch of saffron
3 sprigs of rosemary
Lemon wedges to serve
Salt and freshly ground black pepper
2 dessertspoons (20ml) olive oil

You can use the same method as the risotto, although you can do this on the hob. Sauté the leek in the oil until it starts to colour. Seal the chicken and add the garlic and red pepper for a couple of minutes. Now add the rice and mix around so that each grain is coated with oil. Sprinkle with the saffron and black pepper and then add the stock. Put the rosemary in and cover and simmer for fifteen minutes before adding the seafood and beans. Cover again for about fifteen minutes. Don't be tempted, at this point, to take a peek every couple of minutes to see how it is doing. I always try to get the rice to start to catch so you get dark crunchy scrapings from the bottom of the pan. Serve with lemon wedges.

Focaccia

300g strong bread flour
½ sachet of bread yeast
1 teaspoon sugar
1 pinch of salt
200ml tepid (30 - 40°C) water
6 - 7 runnerbeans, cut into shorter squarer sections, you may need to destring the beans first.
An ample supply of sage leaves

This is a flat loaf. Use a bread machine to make the dough. Turn it out after its first rise onto a floured baking stone or tray and spread it out so that it is about two centimetres thick. Make deep indentations as you push in the sage leaves with the pieces of bean all over the surface. Brush with olive oil and liberally sprinkle with Maldon salt. Leave to rise for 45 minutes before baking at 190°C for about twenty minutes.

Vegetables

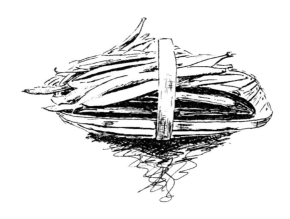

Runner beans and sage with prosciutto

Sage and runner beans are at their best at the same time.

Ingredients (for 4)

500g runner beans, sliced
24 sage leaves
2 shallot sized onions
6 - 8 slices of prosciutto
4 slices from half a lemon and use the remainder for juice
1 tablespoon (15ml) olive oil
Salt and black pepper

Slice beans and very finely chop the sage and onion. Put in a baking dish with the olive oil and mix together by hand. Sprinkle with salt and pepper and place prosciutto and lemon slices on top so as to completely cover the beans and squeeze over the lemon juice. Bake at 200°C for twelve to fifteen minutes. The prosciutto becomes crispy and the beans infuse with the sage steam. Alternatively you can have this as a main meal if you roughly double the quantities. In addition slice tomatoes and throw 25g Gruyère cheese on top. Serve with fresh bread and a crisp white wine in the early autumn sun.

Runner beans and tomato

Ingredients (for 4)

250g ripe tomatoes, chopped
500g runner beans, sliced
1 garlic clove, crushed
Freshly ground black pepper and salt
1 handful of oregano, roughly chopped
1 tablespoon (15ml) olive oil

In a thick bottomed pan soften the garlic in the oil and throw in the tomato, pepper and oregano and gently simmer, stirring occasionally to stop it from sticking. When the tomatoes have melted, about fifteen to twenty minutes, mix in the runner beans to cook. Add salt to taste.

Beans with chorizo and beetroot

Ingredients (for 2)

120g boiled beetroot, cut into batons
60g chorizo, cut into batons
120g runner beans, sliced
1 small onion, thinly sliced
Pepper and salt
2 sprigs of thyme, leaves removed and chopped
1 teaspoon (5ml) of olive oil

Start to sauté the onion in the olive oil, add the chorizo for three to four minutes before adding the beans, beetroot, pepper and thyme and cover, stirring round occasionally, for about five minutes. Great with gamey sausage.

Bean gratin

An improvement on cauliflower cheese and very simple.

Ingredients (for 4)

400g - 600g runner beans, sliced
2 cloves garlic, crushed
Freshly ground black pepper and salt
250ml crème fraiche
125g cheese like Cheddar or Gruyère, finely grated
1 tablespoon (15ml) of sherry or white wine
1 tablespoon of almond flakes

Place the beans in an oven proof dish and sprinkle with the garlic and seasoning. Mix the crème fraiche with the sherry or wine and four fifths (100g) of the cheese and pour this evenly over the beans. Sprinkle over the almonds and the remaining cheese and bake at 180°C until golden brown.

Bean tian with courgette

Ingredients (for 4)

1 tablespoon (15ml) olive oil
1 onion, chopped
2 cloves garlic, crushed
1 red pepper, chopped
125g - 150g courgettes, thinly sliced
125g - 150g runner beans, sliced
4 tomatoes, chopped
50g cooked rice
3 eggs, beaten
1 tablespoon of chopped thyme
2 - 3 tablespoons of chopped parsley
1 tablespoon of grated Parmesan
1 tablespoon of breadcrumbs
Salt and pepper

Sauté onion until soft and add garlic, red pepper, courgette and beans and cook slowly for ten minutes. Remove from the heat. Add tomato, rice, eggs, herbs and salt and pepper, stir well and put into a greased gratin dish. Sprinkle on the breadcrumbs and cheese and bake at 160°C for about 40 - 45 minutes.

Runners with sesame seeds

Ingredients (for 4)

400g - 600g runner beans, sliced
25g butter
2 spring onions, thinly sliced
1 dessertspoon (10ml) juice and grated rind of half a lemon
1 tablespoon sesame seeds, dry fried
Salt and pepper

Steam beans. Sauté the onions in the butter until soft. Stir in lemon juice and rind and add beans, salt and pepper and simmer for 10 minutes. Serve sprinkled with the sesame seeds and a small knob of butter or a drizzle of olive oil.

Beans with winter savory

Ingredients (for 4)

400g - 600g runner beans, sliced
1 garlic clove, crushed
½ teaspoon black pepper
3 - 4 sprigs of winter savory, finely chopped
1 tablespoon (15ml) juice of most of a lemon
2 tablespoons (30ml) olive oil

Steam beans. Heat a serving bowl. Put everything in the bowl and toss. Cover and let it sit for 2 minutes before serving.

Beans with egg and lemon

Ingredients (for 4)

400g runner beans, sliced
1 egg
2 dessertspoons (20ml) juice of one lemon
1 tablespoon of grated Parmesan
1 teaspoon (5ml) olive oil
Salt and black pepper

Steam beans. In a bowl whisk the egg until you get a froth and then whisk in the rest of the ingredients. Put the bowl over a pan of boiling water, whisking all the time until you have a custard-type consistency and immediately remove from the heat and pour over the beans. This can be served hot or cold, but I prefer it cold with cold poached salmon, a bit like a hollandaise sauce.

Bean and potato curry

Ingredients (for 4)

1 onion, finely chopped
1 garlic clove, crushed
1 teaspoon of ground ginger
1 teaspoon of cumin seeds, crushed in a pestle
½ teaspoon of coriander seeds similarly crushed
½ teaspoon salt
½ teaspoon chilli powder
2 cardamon pods
1 teaspoon dried coriander leaf
1 teaspoon of curry powder
½ dessertspoon tomato paste
300g potatoes, 2cm cube
300g runner beans, sliced
2 tomatoes, chopped
1 green pepper, sliced like the beans
3 tablespoons groundnut oil

Fry the onion until it is golden. Add the garlic and ginger and continue to fry for thirty seconds. Turn down the heat and add all the spices except the coriander leaf. Cook for one minute and then stir in the tomato paste followed by the potatoes coating them well in the paste. Add enough water to almost cover. Add the tomatoes and green pepper. Bring to the boil, sprinkle over coriander leaf and simmer for 30 minutes. Now add the beans and continue to cook until the potatoes are soft and the beans are done. Serve with plain boiled rice, nan, raita (or plain yoghurt), popadoms and runner bean chutney, p73.

Thai runner bean curry

Ingredients (for 4)

for the paste
2cm cube of fresh ginger
2 cloves garlic
1 green chilli
1 medium sized red onion
2 ripe tomatoes
1 teaspoon of coriander seeds, dry roasted and ground
1 stalk of lemon grass (optional), finely chopped
and
400g runner beans, sliced
200g baby sweet corn, halved
1 red pepper, sliced like the beans
200ml water or vegetable or chicken stock
1 tablespoon (15ml) Soya sauce
1 tablespoon (15ml) ground nut oil
1 handful of coriander leaves, coarsely chopped
1 teaspoon dark sugar (optional)
1 green chilli, thinly sliced

Make a paste with the first seven ingredients. I use an electric hand blender in a jug. The aroma that rises from the mixture is almost a meal in itself. Fry the paste until the colour starts to change. Stir continuously but do not rush to add the vegetables which, once added, need coating with the paste. Add the water or stock (remember to add salt at this stage if you are using water) and the sugar, if using. Cover pan and simmer until vegetables are tender. This will be about 15 minutes. Serve with the Soya sauce, the second chilli and the fresh coriander with plain boiled rice.

Salads

Marathon runners

Obviously a substitute for Greek salad, for example served with rack of lamb. This is a good way to use lots of beans as they are the bulk of this warm salad.

Ingredients (for 4)

400g - 600g runner beans, sliced
10 black olives, chopped
50g feta, chopped
2 sun-dried tomatoes, chopped
1 tablespoon fresh marjoram, finely chopped
1 tablespoon fresh thyme, finely chopped
Pinch of salt and pepper
1 tablespoon (15ml) olive oil

Mix everything with the freshly steamed beans in a serving bowl.

North African runners

Ingredients (for 4)

400g - 600g runner beans, sliced
1 preserved lemon, chopped, p75
10 black olives, chopped
1 tablespoon toasted pine nuts
1 tablespoon fresh thyme, finely chopped
Salt and black pepper
1 tablespoon (15ml) olive oil

Mix everything with the freshly steamed beans in a serving bowl.

Potato and bean salad

Ingredients (for 4)

300g new potatoes
300g runner beans, sliced
4 spring onions, sliced
A small bunch of parsley, chopped
2 tablespoons (30ml) olive oil
1 teaspoon (5ml) red wine vinegar
Salt and black pepper

Boil the potatoes until soft and cut into quarters. Steam beans. Put everything into a serving bowl and gently toss it. Leave to cool before serving.

Two bean salad with rocket

Ingredients (for 4)

300g runner beans, sliced
1 tin of white beans such as haricot, drained
1 large handful of rocket
a few Parmesan slivers
2 tablespoon French dressing, p 78

Steam beans. Toss everything except the Parmesan in a serving bowl and dress with the cheese.

Preserves

Cumberland bean pickle, a bit like piccalilli and this is enough for six one pound (1lb) jars.

Ingredients

900g runner beans, thinly sliced
450g onions, finely sliced
A pinch of salt
425ml white malt vinegar
50g plain flour (or corn flour)
1 tablespoon mustard powder
½ teaspoon ground black pepper
½ teaspoon ground turmeric
150g white sugar

Put the beans and onions in a pan with a pinch of salt, cover with water and simmer until just tender. In another pan mix together a tablespoon of the vinegar, the flour and the spices to form a smooth paste. Heat gently and mix in the rest of the vinegar as if making a white sauce, stirring all the while with a whisk, and simmer for two to three minutes until the flour is cooked. Add the sugar and mix to make it dissolve. Add the drained beans and onions and bring back to the boil allowing to simmer for ten minutes before putting into sterilized jars.

Pickled beans, traditional

200ml vinegar
100ml water
1 teaspoon black pepper corns
2 teaspoons salt
1 teaspoon allspice berries
500g runner beans, sliced

I have developed what may be called the single jar method, which is a very low effort way of making preserves. However do not deviate from the instructions. It seems to work for most things except jam. Put the ingredients in a large jar, packing the beans as close as possible. Depending on how well you do this you may need to add more or less liquid to just cover the beans. Place the jar on a baking tray and place the lid on top of the jar. DO NOT SCREW IT ON ELSE YOU MAKE A BOMB! Put into a cold oven and set the temperature for 115°C. When bubbles start to rise in the jar you can guarantee that you have killed most of the bugs. Turn off the oven and open the door for about five to ten minutes to allow the jar to start to cool and then tighten the lid. Leave for a couple of weeks before eating.

Pickled beans with tarragon

150ml white wine vinegar
150ml water
Teaspoon black pepper corns
2 teaspoons salt
One sprig of tarragon per jar
500g runner beans, sliced

This is the same method as above.

Bean chutney, single jar method

6 -7 beans, finely sliced
1 medium apple, grated, do this at the last minute otherwise it goes brown
1 small onion, finely sliced
½ teaspoon salt
½ teaspoon mixed spice
2 dessertspoons sultanas
1 small green chilli, finely sliced
2 teaspoons sugar
Malt vinegar

Mix all the ingredients except the vinegar into a bowl. Pack these into a one pound jar and press down well. Pour in the vinegar to just cover. Unlike most things that

I use the single jar method for, this actually needs to cook so the time in the oven is about an hour. Place the jar on a baking tray and place the lid on top of the jar. DO NOT SCREW IT ON ELSE YOU MAKE A BOMB! Put into a cold oven and set the temperature for 115°C. After an hour turn the oven off and fifteen to twenty minutes later screw on the lid and remove from the cooling oven.

Baked tomato ketchup

A home made ketchup to go with anything really but great with bar-b-que'd sausage, freshly steamed beans and crusty bread.

600g tomato, halved
1 onion, sliced
½ red pepper
100ml cider vinegar
15g brown sugar
5mm cinnamon stick
¼ teaspoon mustard seeds
¼ teaspoon coriander seeds
5 - 6 whole cloves
½ teaspoon black pepper
1 bay leaf
1 clove of garlic
¼ teaspoon chilli flakes
Pinch of salt

Place the tomato, onion and pepper in a baking tray. Put the other ingredients in a ramekin and put it on the baking tray with the vegetables. Bake for 30 minutes at 150°C. The vegetables should be soft and the vinegar reduced by about a half and deeply infused with the spices. Empty the ramekin through a sieve onto the vegetables and mix around. When slightly cooler whiz with a hand blender and pour it into a sterilised jar.

Preserved lemons

There are multiple methods for preserved lemons with varied degrees of effort. This, however, is the easiest.

4 unwaxed lemons
2 tablespoons of salt

Cut each of the first three lemons into eights and like a jigsaw pack into a 1lb jar. If there is any room left add the rind of the last lemon to fill the space at the top of the jar. Add the salt and pour over the juice of the last lemon. Place the jar on a baking tray and place the lid on top of the jar. DO NOT SCREW IT ON ELSE YOU MAKE A BOMB! Put into a cold oven and set the temperature for 115°C. When bubbles start to rise in the jar you can guarantee that you have killed most of the bugs and the rest will succumb to the salty acid lemon juice. I think you can effectively keep this for ever now. Turn off the oven and fifteen to twenty minutes later screw on the lid and remove from the cooling oven.

Pickled chillies

Enough home grow chillies to fill a jar when packed carefully
50/50 water and white wine vinegar, you could be more extravagant and use undiluted white wine vinegar

Pack a jar with chillies. When I grow my own I either get a glut or non so this is a worthwhile exercise for the leaner years. Fill up the jar with the fluid to just cover the chillies. Place the jar on a baking tray and place on the lid of the jar. DO NOT SCREW IT ON ELSE YOU MAKE A BOMB! Put into a cold oven and set the temperature for 115°C. When bubbles start to rise in the jar you can guarantee that you have killed most of the bugs and, if the chillies are hot, nothing else will survive. Turn off the oven and fifteen to twenty minutes later screw on the lid and remove from the cooling oven.

Dressings etc

Sage butter

125g salted butter
Handful of sage leaves, finely chopped
Salt and freshly ground black pepper

In a pan soften the butter and vigorously mix in the other ingredients. The butter should not melt or cook the herb. Allow to cool and wrap as a sausage in Clingfilm in the fridge ready to add a knob to your beans.

Anchovy butter

Anchovies and runner beans seem to go so well together.

125g salted butter
6 -7 anchovy fillets

Just soften the butter and mash in the anchovies. Allow to cool and wrap as a sausage in Clingfilm in the fridge ready to add a knob to your beans.

French dressing

A small but tall screw top jar is invaluable for making up these small quantities. I think it is worth making fresh since it is never quite the same each time and adds to variety. Substituting lemon juice instead of the vinegar also provides a change.

1 - 2 tablespoons (15ml - 30ml) olive oil
1 - 2 dessertspoons (10ml - 20ml) white wine vinegar
1 teaspoon smooth French mustard
¼ teaspoon each of black pepper and salt

Shake vigorously in the jar to generate an emulsion. Give another shake before pouring over the salad.

Mint sauce

1 good handful of finely chopped mint leaves, the younger and more tender the better, and not stalks
1 heaped teaspoon (5g) sugar
1 tablespoon (15ml) boiling water
4 tablespoons (60ml) sherry vinegar

Put the sugar and mint in a small jug and add the water to dissolve the sugar. Add the vinegar, how much is really up to you.

Apple sauce

1 large cooking apple, peeled, cored and sliced
2 cloves
1 teaspoon of chopped sage
1 teaspoon (5g) brown sugar
10 - 15g butter

There are no pans, effort or complexity with this method. Just put all the ingredients in a small buttered ovenproof dish and bake in the same oven as your meat until the apple takes on a floury consistency. At 180°C this usually takes half an hour. Mash with a fork and serve in the dish that you cooked it in.

yum yum !

Chicken stock

1 chicken carcass
1 onion, cut in half, don't bother to skin it
1 - 2 carrots, broken in half
1 teaspoons black pepper corns
1 bay leaf
1 sprig of parsley
1 stick of celery

In fact all you need are the first four ingredients really. Put everything into a pan with 1 litre of cold water. Bring to the boil and then simmer very gently for 45 minutes to an hour, covered. Leave to cool, and strain the stock off.

Index

Runner beans and tomatoes, 58
Salad,
    Crunchy bean and chicken salad, 23
    Marathon runners, 67
    North African runners, 68
    Potato and bean, 68
    Two bean salad with rocket, 69
Salmon, baked with runner beans, 26
Sauce,
    Apple, 79
    Mint, 79
    Peanut, 36
Scarlet Emperor, 13
Soup,
    Fresh bean, 21
    Oriental runner bean soup, 22
Streamline, 13
Stir fried chicken with peanut sauce, 36
Tagine aux haricot coccineus, 34
Tapenade, 23
Tian, with beans and courgettes, 60
Tradescant, John, 10
Trout with black pudding and beans, 27
Varieties, 13
Yorkshire pudding, 44

Sorry no puddings

Notes

Old and new money

Weights		Liquid measurements		Oven temperatures		
		1 teaspoon	5ml			
1oz	25g	1 dessertspoon	10ml	115°C	gas mark	½
4oz	100g	1 tablespoon	15ml	150°C	gas mark	2
8oz	225g	¼ pint	150ml	180°C	gas mark	4
1lb	450g	8fl oz	250ml	200°C	gas mark	6
		16fl oz	475ml	220°C	gas mark	7
		1 pint	600ml			

Notes

Notes

Printed in the United Kingdom by
Lightning Source UK Ltd., Milton Keynes
140477UK00001BA/2/P